THAI CUISINE

with Jasmine Rice

Top 25 Thai Dishes

Jasmine Rice with the Compliments of ⬤))))) EastLand

JASMINE RICE

ASIAN BEST ® BRAND

THAI CUISINE
with Jasmine Rice
Top 25 Thai Dishes

ISBN : 974-7588-67-6

Advisor   Pricha Mekhaya
Editor & Co-writer   Wanvisa Niyomsub
Editorial Staff   Nuth Nitibhon
                            Rungrudee Phanichsri
                            Nattana Niyomsub
                            Obchoel Imsabai
                            Rapeepan Jaipakdee
                            C. J. Bruce
Artwork, Design   N.I.S. Media Group Co., Ltd.
& Photography   320 Lat Phrao 94
                            (Town in Town)
                            Wangthonglang, Bangkok
                            10310, Thailand.
                            Tel. (662) 934-4413 ext. 108
                            Fax: (662) 934-4411
                            e-mail: nis@nismediagroup.com
                            website: http://www.sangdad.com

Produced by   ● ●)))) EASTLAND
                            Eastland Food Corporation
                            9475 Gerwig Lane,
                            Columbia, MD. 21046
                            Tel. (410) 381-0710
                            Fax: (410) 381-2079
                            e-mail: eastlandf@aol.com

In the past decade, diners throughout the world have discovered the unique blend of flavors that is Thai cuisine. Thai restaurants are thriving in almost every region of the world thanks to Thai cuisine with its unique and diverse palette of seasonings and its adaptability to local ingredients.

These characteristics provide Thai chefs with the flexibility needed to blend and layer contrasting flavors and add a whole new dimension to Thai cuisine. From Australia to America, Cairo to Caracas, Thai dishes are becoming household names.

Jasmine rice plays an especially important role in Thai cuisine. Its unique aroma and texture help to highlight the many flavors that are essential parts of any Thai meal. Jasmine rice also serves as a moderating element, allowing the palette to savor previously experienced flavors while preparing it to experience new ones. For this reason jasmine rice is the rice best suited for consumption with Thai food as well as many other Asian cuisines.

Identifying and purchasing high quality jasmine rice can be tricky. This booklet is meant to provide an introduction to jasmine rice, to enable the purchaser to correctly identify it and as a guide to the many Thai dishes that can be made and enjoyed with it.

JASMINE RICE

ASIAN BEST BRAND ®

2

INDEX

Rice : Feeding the World — 4

Thailand : Rice Bowl of Asia — 5

Jasmine : The King of Rice — 6

Asian Best Jasmine Rice — 7

How to Cook Rice — 8

Common Use of Herbs and Spices in Thai Cooking — 9

Thai Ingredients and Condiments — 10

Khao Mok Kai (Thai Spiced Chicken with Rice) — 12

Khao Pad Kung Kub Poo
(Fried Rice with Shrimps and Crabmeat) — 14

Khao Mun Kai (Chicken Rice) — 16

Khao Klug Kapi (Shrimp Paste Fried Rice) — 18

Khao Kaphrao Kai Khai Dao
(Fried Basil Chicken with Crisp-fried Egg Rice) — 20

Soup Haang Wua (Oxtail Soup) — 22

Tom Yum Kung (Hot and Sour Soup with Shrimps) — 24

Tom Kha Kai
(Chicken with Galangal and Coconut Soup) — 26

Thai Hot Pot (Thai Soup with Vegetables and Meat) — 28

Kaeng Som Kung (Sour Curry with Shrimps) — 30

Kaeng Khiew Wan Kai
(Green Curry with Chicken and Sweet Basil Leaves) — 32

Panaeng Neua (Beef Sautéed Curry) — 34

Hor Mok Pla (Fish Curry Soufflé) — 36

Yum Woon Sen (Spicy Bean Thread Salad) — 38

Neua Yang Nam Tok (Spicy Grilled Beef) — 40

Yum Talay (Spicy Seafood Salad) — 42

Lap Kai (Savory Chopped Chicken Salad) — 44

Som Tum (Spicy Papaya Salad) — 46

Porpia Tod (Thai Spring Rolls) — 48

Tod Mun Pla (Fried Fish Cake) — 50

Pla Rad Phrik (Fried Sea Bass with Sweet Chili Sauce) — 52

Kai Yang (Thai-Style Grilled Chicken) — 54

Moo Satay (Thai-Style Pork BBQ) — 56

Pad Thai Kung Sod (Fried Noodles with Shrimps) — 58

Kuaytiew Pad Khi Mao Kai
(Spicy Fried Noodles with Chicken) — 60

Asian Best Jasmine Rice — 62

Products Recommended by Eastland — 63

Curry Pastes & Sauce — 64

Rice : Feeding the World

Rice has been one of the world's staple foods for centuries. It plays a significant role in feeding and nourishing more than half of the world's population and is an important source of nutrients such as vitamin B1 and B2, calcium, iron, potassium and folic acid. Rice is also a major source of carbohydrates, the main source of human energy.

Thailand : Rice Bowl of Asia

Rice was first cultivated in Thailand thousands of years ago. Thailand is especially suited for growing rice due to a unique combination of climate and geography. Rice cultivation has become a deeply rooted part of life in Thailand and the country has developed an intimate knowledge of growing and harvesting rice. As a matter of fact, Thailand produces over 100 varieties of rice and exports over 6 million tons to the rest of the world each year. For this reason, Thailand has become known as the **"Rice Bowl of Asia"**.

Jasmine : The King of Rice

Jasmine rice is a naturally occurring species of rice which is renowned for its aroma, texture and taste. It needs very specific weather and soil conditions to achieve these qualities and can only be grown in the Northeastern region of Thailand to achieve its full potential. For this reason, supplies have always been very limited and commanded a premium price over other varieties. In days gone by jasmine rice was so prized that only royalty and the wealthy could afford it. After decades of research and development, scientists and farmers have steadily boosted jasmine rice crop yields so that today it is available to and can be enjoyed by consumers throughout the world.

Asian Best Jasmine Rice

Buying Asian Best Jasmine Rice is the easiest way to ensure that you are getting the best jasmine rice in the world. Due to intense demand and limited supply, buying best quality jasmine rice can be difficult. Many companies will often blend jasmine with inferior varieties of rice to boost volumes available for sale. Some brand names claiming to sell 100% jasmine rice in fact bulk their bagged products with 50% or more of cheap rice varieties to save costs. Quality can vary greatly from brand to brand. From the very beginning, Asian Best has always sought to provide only the highest grade 100% jasmine rice. This has made Asian Best the most popular brand of jasmine rice in the United States.

How to Cook Rice

Having purchased Asian Best Jasmine Rice, preparing fragrant and delicious jasmine rice is easy. Here are three methods.

(a) Using a microwave oven

Put 1 cup of Asian Best Jasmine Rice into a bowl.

Add 1 to 1½ cups of water and stir.

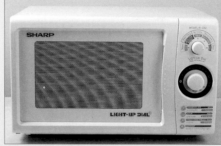

Place in microwave oven and cook at high heat for 4½ minutes. Turn down to medium heat for 5½ minutes. Allow to stand for another 10-15 minutes before serving.

(b) Using pan on stove

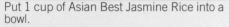

Put 1 cup of Asian Best Jasmine Rice into a bowl.

Add 1 to 1½ cups of water, stir and transfer to a pan.

Cover the pan with a lid. Cook at high heat for 12 minutes. Turn off the heat and allow the pan to stand for 5 minutes before serving.

(c) Using an electric rice cooker

Put 1 cup of Asian Best Jasmine Rice into a rice cooker's pot.

Add 1 to 1½ cups of water per 1 cup of rice or add water in proportion to the additional rice added.

Turn on the electric rice cooker, leave it until it automatically turns off and allow to stand for 10 minutes before serving.

To cook Jasmine Rice perfectly the ratio of rice to water must be correct. Failure to use the correct rice/water ratio will lead to the cooked rice becoming too soft or too hard.

1. Jasmine rice is only harvested once a year during November/December and is usually shipped to reach the US market by late December.

2. The moisture content of packaged rice varies between 14% and 10% depending on the time which has elapsed between harvesting and consumption.

3. To obtain optimal cooking results add water to rice in accordance with the cooking instructions printed on each package.

4. Microwave cooking requires a little less water than other cooking methods while stove cooking may use a little more.

Whichever method of rice cooking that you use will obtain the same result.

Common Use of **Herbs and Spices** in Thai Cooking

Holy Basil
(Kaphrao)
Two types are used in Thai cooking: green and red basil. The latter is more fragrant and spicier.

Coriander
(Phak Chi)
The plant is grown for its leaves, roots and seeds. Pick those with fresh light green leaves with roots attached.

Sweet Basil
(Horapha)
Sweet basil has dark green leaves with red stems. Its leaves are slightly thicker than holy basil and have their own distinctive flavor.

Kaffir Lime
(Makrut)
A Thai herb valued for its zest and the unbeatable aroma of its leaves. The leaves are added to Thai dishes to give aroma. The zest is sliced and pounded into curry paste.

Lemon Grass
(Takhrai)
One of the herbs most frequently used in Thai cuisine ranging from salads to soups to curries.

Garlic
(Krathiem)
Thai garlic has small cloves with a rather soft skin but a strong aroma.

Dried Chili
(Phrik Haeng)
Both spur and hot chilies are used. Dried hot chilies are normally roasted then grounded and used as a seasoning.

Hot Chili
(Phrik Khi Nu)
Small but very spicy hot chili. Use only those with the stems still on.

Shallot
(Hom Daeng)
Small zesty red or yellow onions. Both have a strong smell and flavor but the yellow ones are sweeter in taste.

Galangal
(Kha)
A species of the ginger family. It has a pungency and tang, unlike common ginger.

Wild Ginger
(Krachai)
The fresh plump roots are juicy and have a strong aroma.

Ginger
(Khing)
Two kinds are used in Thai cooking, young ginger is usually sliced and sprinkled over steamed fish. The mature plants with a stronger flavor are best enjoyed in sauces.

9

Thai Ingredients and Condiments

Green Curry Paste
(Kaeng Khiew Wan)
Prepared from an array of herbs and fresh green chilies. Green curry paste is used mainly in chicken curry or Kaeng Khiew Wan Kai.

Red Curry Paste
(Kaeng Daeng)
Hot and spicy, this red curry paste blends typical Thai flavors such as dried red chilies and lemon grass. This paste is used particularly with beef and chicken.

Sour Curry Paste
(Kaeng Som)
This paste is made with dried chili, onion, fish, and tamarind juice, which give it a unique sour taste.

Panaeng Curry Paste
(Panaeng)
Panaeng is Thai curry paste made with shrimp paste, kaffir lime, red chili, sweet basil, lemon grass and galangal. Panaeng curry is richer and sweeter than red and green curry pastes.

Tom Yum Paste
(Tom Yum)
A mild blend of spiciness and sourness accented by the delicate aroma and flavor of lemon grass, citrus leaves, and natural herbs. Tom Yum paste can be used when cooking with chicken or seafood.

Pad Thai Sauce
(Pad Thai)
A popular blend of tamarind juice with herbs and spices to complement Thai style fried rice noodles.

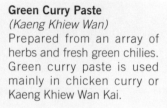

Kaphrao Paste
(Pad Kaphrao)
A fragrant, delicious mix of Thai chili paste and holy basil leaves. This paste can be used with any kind of meat to create a simple, authentic Thai meal.

Peanut Sauce
(Satay Sauce)
Thai peanut sauce is made by cooking ground roasted peanuts in coconut milk with spices and herbs and then seasoning with fish sauce, shrimp paste, palm sugar and tamarinds.

Roasted Chili Paste
(Nam Phrik Phao)
A mixture of chilies, shallots, garlic, dried shrimp and palm sugar which is stir-fried until fragrant. It can be spread on bread or mixed with rice.

Concentrate Tamarind Juice
(Nam Makham Piak)
Tamarind juice comes from the fruit of the tropical tamarind tree. Sour tamarind juice is often used to lend sourness to Thai dishes.

Sweet Chili Sauce
(Nam Jim Kai)
Sweet chili sauce is slightly spicy and sweet. This sauce is especially popular in Thailand and is used with grilled chicken and sticky rice or any deep fried foods.

Spring Roll Sauce
(Nam Jim Porpia)
Spring roll sauce is sweet and sour, with a touch of chili. Yellow in color, with slivers of turnip and carrot, it is perfect with crispy fried spring rolls.

Thai Ingredients and Condiments

Coconut Milk
(Kathi)
Coconut milk is made from fresh coconuts and water. It should be fragrant and have a naturally sweet and nutty flavor. Higher grades of coconut milk have higher coconut fat content.

Thin Soy Sauce
(See-eiw Khao)
Made from soybeans, flour, salt and water, thin soy sauce is a light clear brown liquid which adds a wonderful taste to a simple broth or a stir-fried dish.

Seasoning Sauce
(Sauce Prung Ros)
A seasoned soy sauce which adds more flavor to dishes than regular soy sauce.

Oyster Sauce
(Nam Mun Hoy)
Oyster sauce is a thick, brown, richly flavored sauce. It adds extra flavor to meat, fish, poultry and vegetable dishes, particularly stir-fried dishes.

Chili Sauce
(Sri Raja)
Sharp and hot, chili sauce is very useful as a marinade as well as a general purpose cooking sauce. It is one of the most popular dipping sauces in Thailand.

Fish Sauce
(Nam Pla)
A pale amber liquid brewed from fish or shrimps mixed with salt used extensively in Thai cooking. It is a thin sauce with strong flavor and aroma.

Bamboo Shoot
(Nor Mai)
The young shoots of bamboo plants, used in stir-fried dishes and curries. They are widely available in cans, sliced or whole.

Straw Mushroom
(Hed Fang)
A common mushroom found throughout Southeast Asia. Straw Mushrooms are used in various kinds of soups, curries and stir-fried dishes. They are conveniently available in cans.

Palm Sugar
(Nam Tan Peep)
Palm sugar is made by boiling the sap of coconut palms or toddy palms so that the liquid solidifies into a cake. In Thai cuisine, it is preferred for its mild sweetness.

Shrimp Paste
(Kapi)
Shrimp paste is made from ground shrimps and is used in curry pastes, sauces, soups and stir-fries. The paste is fragrant and salty.

Bean Thread
(Woon Sen)
Bean thread noodles are made from mung bean flour. They are only available dried and are used in soups, some stir-fried dishes and spicy salad dishes.

Rice Noodles
(Pad Thai Noodles)
Rice noodles are flat white noodles made from rice flour and cut into strips of various sizes.

saffron | cumin | mint leaf

cardamom | shallot | cinnamon

Khao Mok Kai
(Thai Spiced Chicken with Rice)

Rice cooked with spices, milk, butter, raisins, green peas, cashew nuts and chicken, served with sweet and sour sauce.

Ingredients (for 6 persons)

3	cups	rice
6		chicken drumsticks
2	tbsp	green peas
1/2	cup	mint leaves, coarsely chopped
1/4	cup	raisins
1	cup	fried sliced shallot
2	tbsp	roasted cashew nuts, coarsely chopped
1	tbsp	roasted cumin
1		cinnamon stick, 2" long
1/2	tsp	ground cloves
1/2	tsp	ground cardamom
1	tsp	saffron
2	tbsp	sugar
3	tsp	salt
3/4	cup	yogurt
1/2	cup	unsweetened evaporated milk
2	cups	water
1/4	cup	butter
1/2	cup	vegetable oil
Garnish:		red spur chilies, lettuce and spring onion
Sauce		Khao Mok Kai sauce (see p. 64)

JASMINE RICE

ASIAN BEST BRAND

Preparation

- Combine yogurt, unsweetened evaporated milk, mint leaves, fried shallots, cumin, sugar, 1/2 teaspoon of saffron and 2 teaspoons of salt. Divide into 2 portions and set aside.
- Rub the chicken drumsticks with 1/2 teaspoon of salt, and fry in 1/2 cup of oil mixed with 1/4 cup of butter until golden brown. Place in a pot and mix thoroughly with one portion of the mixture from step 1. Save the oil.
- Add water to the remaining saffron, strain and pour over jasmine rice. Add the cloves, cardamom, cinnamon stick and 1/2 teaspoon of salt. Boil until the rice is nearly done, then add raisins, cashew nuts and green peas; stir well.
- Divide jasmine rice into 2 portions. Place one portion in a pot, arrange fried chicken over the rice and cover the chicken with the remaining rice. Pour the other portion of the mixture from step 1 over the rice.
- Pour oil, left over from the chicken drumsticks, into pot. Cover and cook for another 30 minutes, or until done. Spoon the rice and chicken onto a dish. Garnish with shredded chilies, lettuce and spring onion. Serve hot with Khao Mok Kai sauce. (see p. 64)

Divide the mixture into 2 portions.

Cook rice with saffron water and spices.

Add raisins, cashew nuts and peas when the rice is nearly done.

Take out half of the rice, add chicken in and add the rice back.

●●▷))) EastLand
Serving the Best

shrimp   garlic   crabmeat

spring onion   thin soy sauce   egg

Khao Pad Kung Kub Poo
(Fried Rice with Shrimps and Crabmeat)

Fried rice with shrimps and crabmeat. This quick and easy meal is a household favorite in Thailand.

Preparation

- Fry garlic in oil until fragrant, add an egg and stir, follow with shrimps and fry until done. Add steamed rice and stir, followed by the crabmeat (reserve some crabmeat for garnish). Season with sugar, soy sauce and pepper, continue cooking and stirring constantly until cooked.
- Spoon jasmine rice mixture onto a dish, sprinkle sliced spring onion over the rice. Garnish with coriander sprigs and shredded chilies. Serve with spring onion, lime wedge and sliced cucumbers.

Note: You can use your choice of meat (chicken, pork).

Ingredients   (for 2 persons)

2	cups	cooked rice
6		medium size shrimps
1/4	cup	cooked crabmeat
1		egg
1	tbsp	sliced spring onion
1	tsp	chopped garlic
1/2	tsp	ground pepper
1/2	tsp	sugar
1	tbsp	thin soy sauce (see p. 11)
3	tbsp	vegetable oil

Fresh vegetables: spring onion, cucumber and lime wedge

Garnish: coriander sprigs and shredded red spur chilies

Fry garlic until fragrant, add an egg, and stir well.

Add shrimps and fry until done.

Add crabmeat into the pan.

Season with thin soy sauce.

JASMINE RICE

ASIAN BEST BRAND

●●))))) EASTLAND

Serving the Best

14

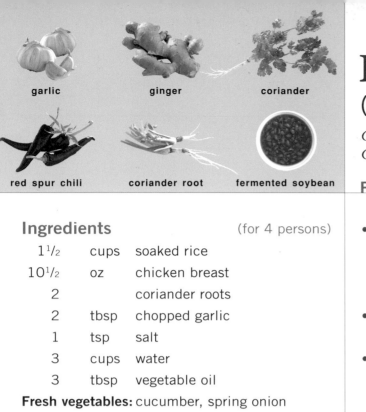

garlic   ginger   coriander

red spur chili   coriander root   fermented soybean

Khao Mun Kai
(Chicken Rice)

Cooked rice with chicken stock, topped with boiled chicken and served with sauce. Good for breakfast or lunch.

Ingredients   (for 4 persons)

1¹/₂	cups	soaked rice
10¹/₂	oz	chicken breast
2		coriander roots
2	tbsp	chopped garlic
1	tsp	salt
3	cups	water
3	tbsp	vegetable oil

Fresh vegetables: cucumber, spring onion

Garnish: lettuce, spring onion

Sauce

1/2	tbsp	red spur chili, ground
1	tbsp	ginger, ground
3	tbsp	fermented soybean
1	tsp	sugar
1	tbsp	vinegar
1	tsp	sweet soy sauce
		coriander leaves for garnish

JASMINE RICE

ASIAN BEST ® BRAND

Preparation

- Boil water, add salt and coriander roots, then add the chicken breast. When the water boils again, turn down the heat and skim the froth from the surface of the stock. Simmer for 15 minutes or until the broth becomes clear. Remove from the heat and strain. This will give 2¹/₂ cups of stock. Slice the chicken breast into pieces.
- Stir-fry garlic in vegetable oil until fragrant, add soaked jasmine rice and stir for a few minutes. Transfer mixture to a pot, add the chicken stock. Cook for 20 minutes.
- To serve, spoon the cooked jasmine rice into a mold, pressing firmly. Unmold the rice on a serving dish, arrange the chicken on one side. Garnish with lettuce, spring onion. Serve with sliced cucumbers, spring onion and ginger sauce.

Sauce

- Pound the fermented soybeans into a fine paste and then stir in sweet soy sauce, vinegar, sugar, ginger and chili. Garnish with coriander leaves.

Add the chicken into boiling hot water.

Strain the chicken stock.

Fry soaked rice with garlic.

Steam the rice until done.

EastLand
Serving the Best

16

shrimp paste   palm sugar   fish sauce

green mango   shallot   dried shrimp

Khao Klug Kapi
(Shrimp Paste Fried Rice)

Fried rice with shrimp paste topped with shredded omelette, crisp-fried dried shrimp, sliced green mango, sweetened pork, chili and sliced shallots. Well-known in central Thailand. Usually served with soup.

Preparation

- Fry shallots in oil over medium heat until fragrant. Add palm sugar, fish sauce and water, simmer until slightly thickened. Add pork, stir until done. Turn down heat, continue to simmer until the pork absorbs all the liquid and appears glossy. Turn off the heat.
- Heat 1/4 cup of oil in a pan over medium heat. Fry dried shrimp until crisp, remove from the oil.
- Fry shallots in oil until fragrant, add shrimp paste and stir well. Season with sugar and fish sauce. Transfer the mixture to a mixing bowl, add cooked rice and mix together.
- Spoon the jasmine rice mixture onto a serving dish and decorate with shredded omelette, sweetened pork, crisp-fried dried shrimps, sliced mango, sliced Thai chilies, sliced shallots and coriander leaves.

Ingredients

(for 3 persons)

3	cups	cooked rice
1	tbsp	shrimp paste (see p. 11)
1 1/2	tbsp	chopped shallots
1 1/2	tbsp	palm sugar
1	tsp	fish sauce (see p. 11)
2	tbsp	vegetable oil
1/4	cup	vegetable oil, for deep-frying
3	tbsp	dried shrimps
Garnish:		coriander leaves

Sweetened pork

5	oz	pork, cut into small pieces
1	tbsp	chopped shallots
1/4	cup	palm sugar (see p. 11)
1	tbsp	fish sauce (see p. 11)
1	tbsp	water
1	tbsp	vegetable oil

Condiments

6	tbsp	sweetened pork
3	tbsp	fried dried shrimps
3	tbsp	sliced green mango
3	tsp	sliced Thai chilies
3	tbsp	sliced shallots
1		coarsely shredded omelette

JASMINE RICE

ASIAN BEST BRAND

Simmer the sauce until slightly thickened.

Add the pork, continue simmering over low heat.

Season the shrimp paste with palm sugar.

Mix the rice with shrimp paste mixture until combined.

EastLand
Serving the Best

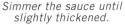

18

holy basil leaf   egg   fish sauce

Thai chili   chicken   garlic

Khao Kaphrao Kai Khai Dao
(Fried Basil Chicken with Crisp-fried Egg Rice)

Rich in herbs, this simple dish is a favorite in Thailand.

Ingredients   (for 2 persons)

3	cups	cooked rice
1	cup	chopped chicken
2		eggs
1	cup	holy basil leaves
1-5		Thai chilies
2	tbsp	chopped garlic
1	tsp	sugar
1	tbsp	fish sauce (see p. 11)
1	tbsp	oyster sauce (see p. 11)
3	tbsp	oil, for stir-frying
1	cup	oil, for deep-frying eggs
Garnish:		crisp-fried holy basil sprigs and Thai chilies

Preparation

- Pound garlic and chilies until coarse, then set aside.
- Heat 1 cup of oil in a pan, fry eggs, one at a time until golden and crispy around the edges. Set aside.
- Heat 3 tablespoons of oil in a pan, add the pounded garlic and chilies from step 1 and fry until fragrant. Add chicken and stir-fry until done.
- Add sugar, fish sauce and oyster sauce. Turn heat to high, add holy basil leaves and stir.
- Serve hot with cooked jasmine rice, garnish with basil sprigs, Thai chilies and the crisp-fried egg.

Note: If raw spices are difficult to obtain, use Maesri Kaphrao paste.

Blend garlic and Thai chilies together.

Fry the mixture in oil until fragrant, add chicken, stir well.

Add fish sauce and oyster sauce.

Add holy basil leaves and stir well until done.

JASMINE RICE

ASIAN BEST BRAND

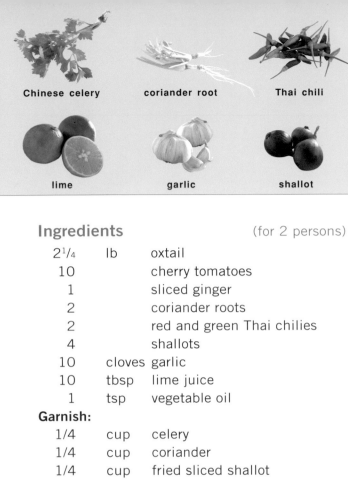

Chinese celery   coriander root   Thai chili

lime   garlic   shallot

Soup Haang Wua
(Oxtail Soup)

Delicious oxtail soup. Serve with jasmine rice.

Ingredients

			(for 2 persons)
2¼	lb	oxtail	
10		cherry tomatoes	
1		sliced ginger	
2		coriander roots	
2		red and green Thai chilies	
4		shallots	
10	cloves	garlic	
10	tbsp	lime juice	
1	tsp	vegetable oil	

Garnish:

1/4	cup	celery
1/4	cup	coriander
1/4	cup	fried sliced shallot

Soup stock

3		2" long cinnamon sticks
7		cloves
7		cardamoms
7	cloves	crushed garlic
1	tsb	crushed peppercorn
2	tbsp	salt
8	cups	water

JASMINE RICE

ASIAN BEST BRAND ®

Preparation

- Wash the oxtail thoroughly and place it in a pot with enough water to cover. Add 2 tablespoons of salt and boil over medium heat until cooked and tender. Drain and set aside.
- Pound shallots, garlic, chilies, coriander roots and ginger into a fine paste. Sauté in oil over medium heat until fragrant, remove from the pan.
- Pour 8 cups of water into a pot. Add soup ingredients and boil until fragrant. Add the sautéed paste from step 2.
- Continue boiling for a few minutes then add the oxtail. Follow with tomatoes, lime juice and a pinch of salt.
- Spoon the soup into a serving bowl, sprinkle sliced celery, coriander and crisp-fried shallot on top. Serve hot as starter or with fragrant cooked jasmine rice.

Boil the oxtail until cooked and tender.

Sauté the paste in oil over medium heat until crispy.

Add 8 cups of water into the pot, add all spices.

Add the cooked oxtail in.

Thai chili kaffir lime leaf lime
straw mushroom lemon grass shrimp

Tom Yum Kung
(Hot and Sour Soup with Shrimps)

A hot and spicy soup and a favorite among Thai people. A clear broth with mush-rooms, shrimps and the distinctive scent of Thai herbs such as lemon grass, kaffir lime leaves and lime juice.

Preparation

Ingredients   (for 3 persons)

9		shrimps
7	oz	halved straw mushrooms (see p. 11)
9		Thai chilies, lightly crushed
1		lemon grass stem
5		kaffir lime leaves
1	tbsp	roasted chili paste (see p. 10)
2	tbsp	fish sauce (see p. 11)
3	tbsp	lime juice
4	cups	chicken stock
Garnish:		kaffir lime leaves, slices of lemon grass and Thai chilies

- Remove the outer layer of the lemon grass stems and wash thoroughly. Cut off stems $2^{1}/_{2}$" from base and slice diagonally into 1/4" pieces.
- Boil chicken stock, add lemon grass and continue boiling until fragrant. Then add straw mushrooms and shrimps and boil until cooked.
- Add fish sauce, lime juice, chili paste, kaffir lime leaves and chilies. Boil once more.
- Pour *Tom Yum Kung* into a serving bowl, garnish with kaffir lime leaves, slices of lemon grass and chilies. Serve hot with fragrant cooked jasmine rice.

Note: If raw spices are difficult to obtain, use Maesri Tom Yum paste.

JASMINE RICE

ASIAN BEST ® BRAND

Prepare shrimps for Tom Yum Soup.

Slice the lemon grass diagonally.

When the mushrooms are almost done, add the shrimps.

Season and stir well.

Thai chili   kaffir lime leaf   lime

young galangal   chicken breast   coriander

Tom Kha Kai
(Chicken with Galangal and Coconut Soup)

A favorite soup with chicken and Thai herbs in coconut milk. A mouth watering blend of sourness and sweetness. Enjoy with jasmine rice.

Ingredients   (for 2 persons)

1	lb	chicken breast
7	oz	halved straw mushrooms (see p. 11)
1/3	cup	young galangal, sliced
3	cups	coconut milk
5-7		Thai chilies, lightly crushed
3		kaffir lime leaves
1	tsp	salt
1	tsp	sugar
1½	tbsp	fish sauce (see p. 11)
3	tbsp	lime juice
Garnish:		coriander (optional), kaffir lime leaves, Thai chilies and sliced young galangal

Preparation

- Cut the chicken into bite-size pieces.
- Boil 2 cups of coconut milk, using medium heat. Add the chicken, salt and galangal and continue boiling until the chicken is tender, then add the remaining cup of coconut milk, mushrooms and kaffir lime leaves.
- Season with sugar, lime juice, fish sauce and Thai chilies, then turn off the heat.
- Spoon the soup into a serving bowl, garnish with kaffir lime leaves, Thai chilies and young galangal. Serve with cooked jasmine rice.

Cut the chicken into bite-size pieces.

Add galangal and chicken into the boiling coconut milk.

Add the remaining coconut milk and straw mushrooms.

Add the kaffir lime leaves and Thai chilies.

JASMINE RICE

ASIAN BEST BRAND ®

shrimp egg squid

Chinese watercress baby corn Chinese cabbage

shiitake mushroom Chinese celery suki sauce

Thai Hot Pot
(Thai Soup with Vegetables and Meat)

A popular dish in central Thailand. This is a family favorite made with a variety of meat and fresh vegetables. The suki sauce is made from a mixture of sesame, spices and chilies.

Preparation

- Pour the chicken stock into a pot and place over medium heat until boiling. Add the beaten egg and stir well then add your choice of meat and vegetables to the chicken stock and boil until cooked. Serve steaming hot with suki sauce.
- Add more soup if needed.

Note: A hot pot can be used in which case the method of preparation indicated by the illustrations and directions provided below should be followed.

Ingredients   (for 4 persons)

1¹⁄₂	cups	suki sauce
15	cups	chicken stock

Meat & vegetables of your choice

and as much as you need:

shrimps, squid,

beef tenderloin,

fish balls, tofu, eggs,

Chinese watercress,

Chinese celery,

Chinese cabbage, carrots,

fresh shiitake mushroom,

baby corn, bean thread

(see p. 11), etc.

JASMINE RICE

ASIAN BEST BRAND ®

Lightly beat the egg(s) and pour into a pot of boiling hot chicken stock.

Add vegetables and boil until cooked.

Add the meat to the chicken stock. When cooked, serve in a bowl.

Add suki sauce and serve steaming hot.

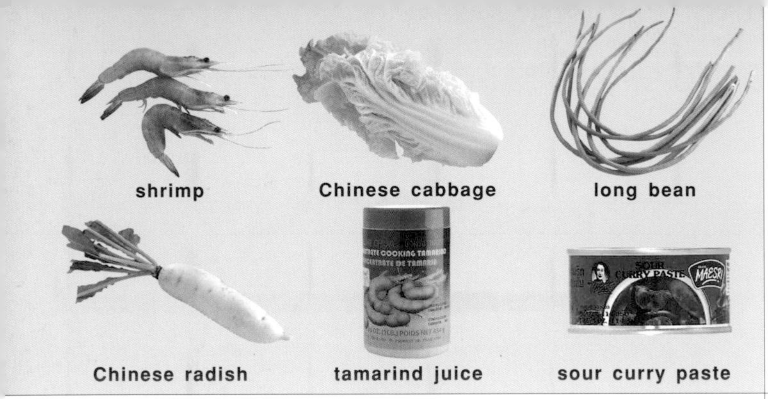

Image labels (top left)

shrimp

Chinese cabbage

long bean

Chinese radish

tamarind juice

sour curry paste

Kaeng Som Kung
(Sour Curry with Shrimps)

Hot and sour red curry soup. A delicious blend of curry and vegetables flavored with tamarind juice.

Ingredients

(for 2 persons)

10		shrimps
3½	oz	sliced Chinese radish
3½	oz	sliced carrot
5	leaves	Chinese cabbage, cut into 1 inch lengths
1	tbsp	canned sour curry paste (see p. 10)
5		long beans, cut into 1 inch lengths
10		Chinese watercress tips
1	tbsp	palm sugar (see p. 11)
3	tbsp	fish sauce (see p. 11)
3	tbsp	tamarind juice (see p. 10)
2	cups	water

Preparation

- Bring water to the boil. Add the sour curry paste, stir well. When boiling again, add carrots and Chinese radish and continue boiling until done. Add beans and Chinese watercress tips, followed by the Chinese cabbage, once the beans are done.
- Season with tamarind juice, fish sauce and palm sugar. Cook over low heat for 5 minutes before adding shrimps. Cook until the shrimps are done. Turn off the heat.
- Serve with fragrant cooked jasmine rice.

Clean the shrimps, prepare for cooking.

Add sour curry paste into a pot of boiling water.

Add carrot, Chinese radish and boil until done. Then add beans, Chinese watercress tips and Chinese cabbage, respectively.

Add shrimps and cook until done. Turn off the heat.

JASMINE RICE

ASIAN BEST BRAND ®

●●))))) EASTLAND
Serving the Best

green curry paste   kaffir lime leaf   red spur chili

eggplant   coconut   sweet basil leaf

Kaeng Khiew Wan Kai
(Green Curry with Chicken and Sweet Basil Leaves)

Chicken in creamy coconut soup with eggplants and green curry paste. A popular Thai curry best served with cooked jasmine rice.

Ingredients   (for 4 persons)

14	oz	chicken breast, cut into bite-size pieces
3	cups	coconut milk
3	tbsp	green curry paste (see p. 10)
5	oz	small eggplants
2		kaffir lime leaves, torn into pieces
1/4	cup	sweet basil leaves
2-3		red spur chilies, sliced diagonally
1½-2	tbsp	fish sauce (see p. 11)
1½	tsp	palm sugar (see p. 11)
1	tbsp	vegetable oil
Garnish:		sweet basil sprigs and red spur chili

Preparation

- Stir-fry the curry paste in vegetable oil over medium heat until fragrant. Turn down the heat and gradually add 1 cup of coconut milk; fry until a film of oil surfaces.
- Add chicken and kaffir lime leaves and stir-fry until cooked. Add the remaining coconut milk and stir. Season with fish sauce and sugar. When the mixture comes to the boil, add small eggplants and boil until they are done. Sprinkle with sweet basil leaves and chilies then remove from the heat.
- Spoon the curry into a serving bowl, garnish with sweet basil sprigs and chilies. Enjoy with cooked jasmine rice.

Gradually add small amount of coconut milk, and stir-fry with the curry paste.

Add chicken and kaffir lime leaves, stir thoroughly.

Add the remaining coconut milk.

When the small eggplants are cooked through, sprinkle with sweet basil leaves and red chilies.

JASMINE RICE

ASIAN BEST BRAND

 **EastLand**
Serving the Best

32

red spur chili | kaffir lime leaf | beef tenderloin

coconut | roasted peanut | panaeng curry paste

Panaeng Neua
(Beef Sautéed Curry)

Originally from central Thailand, this is a spicy stir-fried beef curry with coconut milk. Served with cooked jasmine rice.

Preparation

- Heat 1/2 cup of coconut milk until the oil surfaces, then add the Panaeng curry paste.
- Add the beef and fry for 3 minutes, then add the rest of the coconut milk.
- Season with salt, fish sauce, sugar and ground roasted peanuts and simmer for 5 minutes until beef is tender. Add the kaffir lime leaves and chilies. Turn off the heat.
- Spoon into a serving bowl, garnish with kaffir lime leaves and chilies and serve hot with cooked jasmine rice.

Ingredients

(for 2 persons)

7	oz	beef tenderloin, cut into bite-size pieces
1	cup	coconut milk
1½	tbsp	panaeng curry paste (see p. 10)
2		sliced red spur chilies
6		kaffir lime leaves
3	tbsp	ground roasted peanuts
1/8	tsp	salt
2	tsp	sugar
1	tbsp	fish sauce (see p. 11)
Garnish:		kaffir lime leaves and red spur chilies

JASMINE RICE

ASIAN BEST®BRAND

Stir-fry the curry paste with the coconut milk.

Add the remaining coconut milk to the sautéed beef.

Add ground peanuts.

Simmer until the beef is tender, sprinkle with kaffir lime leaves and red chilies.

●●))))) EASTLAND
Serving the Best

34

egg   sweet basil leaf   coriander leaf

kaffir lime leaf   coconut   red spur chili

Hor Mok Pla
(Fish Curry Soufflé)

Steamed fish blended with red curry paste and sweet basil leaves. A popular dish from central Thailand which can be served as an appetizer or main dish with cooked jasmine rice.

Preparation

Ingredients

(for 4 persons)

1	lb	fish fillet
2	cups	coconut milk
1	tsp	rice flour
1		egg
3	tbsp	fish sauce (see p. 11)
1	cup	sweet basil leaves, blanched
1/2	cup	sweet basil leaves, fresh
1/2	cup	coriander leaves
3	tbsp	kaffir lime leaves, finely shredded
1	tbsp	red spur chili, shredded

Curry paste

2-5		dried red chilies, soaked
3	tbsp	chopped garlic
1	tsp	kaffir lime rind, finely chopped
2	tbsp	lemongrass, finely chopped
1	tbsp	galangal, finely chopped
2	tsp	coriander roots, finely chopped
4		peppercorns
1/2	tsp	salt
1	tsp	shrimp paste (see p. 11)
2	tbsp	red curry paste (see p. 10)

Note: To make it simpler, use 1 tbsp of instant red curry paste.

JASMINE RICE

ASIAN BEST BRAND

- To make the curry paste, pound all the curry paste ingredients together.
- Cut fish fillet into bite-size pieces.
- Add rice flour into 1/2 cup of coconut milk, stir until thoroughly mixed. Place over low heat, stir until the mixture is cooked. Remove from the heat.
- Mix 1 cup of coconut milk with the curry paste. Add fish and stir well. Add an egg and fish sauce and stir again while gradually adding the remaining coconut milk.
- Add 1/2 cup of sweet basil leaves, 1 tablespoon of coriander and 2 tablespoons of kaffir lime leaves to the mixture and stir until the ingredients are well-blended.
- Line the bottom of a serving bowl with blanched sweet basil leaves and spoon the mixture from Step 5 over the leaves. Arrange the bowls on a steamer tray and steam over boiling water for 15 minutes using high heat. Remove from the heat.
- Top with coconut milk topping from step 3 and sprinkle with chopped coriander, kaffir lime leaves and shredded chili. Then steam for 1 more minute and remove from heat. Serve with cooked jasmine rice.

Combine the fish with the curry paste and coconut milk, stir lightly.

Add the remaining coconut milk.

Sprinkle with sweet basil leaves, coriander leaves and kaffir lime leaves, and stir.

Spoon the mixture into a bowl.

● ◑)))) **EastLand**
Serving the Best

bean thread   dried shrimp   Chinese celery

shrimp   onion   lettuce

Yum Woon Sen
(Spicy Bean Thread Salad)

Bean threads with a choice of meat in a spicy lime dressing. A good appetizer and delicious with cooked jasmine rice.

Preparation

- To make the spicy salad dressing, chop garlic, red and green chilies, and combine with fish sauce, lime juice and sugar in a bowl, stir gently to mix.
- Boil the bean thread for 2 minutes and rinse. Transfer to the mixing bowl.
- Add the boiled pork, shrimps, and sliced celery followed by the salad dressing and onion and mix well.
- Serve spicy bean thread salad on a lettuce-lined plate garnished with sprigs of celery.

Ingredients   (for 2 persons)

1$\frac{1}{2}$	cup	soaked bean thread, (2$\frac{1}{2}$ inch cut)
1/2	cup	boiled pork (or chicken)
8		boiled shrimps
1/4	cup	onion, sliced
2	tbsp	celery, cut into short lengths
Garnish:		lettuce and sprigs of celery

Lime dressing

1	tbsp	red & green spur chilies, chopped
3	tbsp	fish sauce (see p. 11)
4	tbsp	lime juice
2	tbsp	sugar
1	tbsp	minced garlic

JASMINE RICE

ASIAN BEST BRAND ®

Mix garlic, chilies, fish sauce, lime juice and sugar in a bowl.   *Boil bean threads for 2 minutes and rinse out.*   *Put all the ingredients into a mixing bowl.*   *Add the spicy dressing, toss lightly.*

EASTLAND
Serving the Best

ground roasted rice   spring onion   lime

shallot   mint leaf   fish sauce

Neua Yang Nam Tok
(Spicy Grilled Beef)

Grilled beef mixed with spicy salad dressing, this is a northeastern dish but enjoyed in every region. Served with fresh vegetables.

Preparation

- Slice the beef into pieces about 1 inch thick for grilling.
- Grill the beef over high heat.
- Slice grilled beef into bite-size pieces and place in a mixing bowl. Season with fish sauce, lime juice, chili flakes and ground roasted rice.
- Add the sliced shallots, spring onion, saw-leaf coriander and mint leaves.
- Garnish with mint sprigs, red chili, shallot, spring onion, Chinese cabbage and saw-leaf coriander. Serve with cabbage and long beans. Serve accompanied by cooked fragrant jasmine rice.

Ingredients
(for 3 persons)

7	oz	beef tenderloin
1/2	cup	mint leaves
1	tbsp	chopped spring onion
1	tbsp	chopped saw-leaf corainder
1	tbsp	roasted dried chili flakes
2	tbsp	sliced shallot
1	tbsp	ground roasted rice
3	tbsp	fish sauce (see p. 11)
3	tbsp	lime juice

Fresh vegetables: long beans, cabbage

Garnish: mint sprigs, red chili, sliced shallot, chopped saw-leaf coriander, chopped spring onion, and Chinese cabbage

JASMINE RICE

ASIAN BEST BRAND ®

Slice the beef into pieces about 1 inch thick.

Grill the beef over high heat until done.

Add ground roasted rice into sliced grilled beef.

Add shallot, spring onion, coriander and mint leaves, stir gently.

shrimp

squid

mussel

onion

Chinese celery

Thai chili

Yum Talay
(Spicy Seafood Salad)

Assorted seafood blended with lime juice, fish sauce, garlic, chilies and sugar. Absolutely delightful as an appetizer or with jasmine rice.

Preparation

- To make the spicy salad dressing: Pound garlic and chilies together. Season with fish sauce, sugar and lime juice. Stir until the sugar dissolves.
- Clean the shrimps, remove shells and heads but keep the tails intact. Blanch in boiling hot water until done.
- Blanch the mussels and discard the shells.
- Clean the squid, make a criss-cross pattern with a knife, then cut into bite-size pieces. Blanch in boiling water for 1-3 minutes. Steam crab legs and fish meat until done.
- Place all the cooked seafood into a bowl. Pour the spicy dressing over the seafood and toss gently. Add onion and celery and toss again.
- Garnish with celery sprigs. Serve immediately accompanied by cooked jasmine rice.

Ingredients

(for 4 persons)

8		shrimps
7	oz	sea bass
15		mussels
7	oz	squid
4		crab legs
1/2	cup	Chinese celery, cut into 1" long strips
1	cup	onion, cut into wedges
Garnish:		Chinese celery sprigs

Dressing

4-5		Thai chilies
9	cloves	garlic
4	tbsp	lime juice
3	tbsp	fish sauce (see p. 11)
1	tsp	sugar

(see p. 11)

JASMINE RICE

ASIAN BEST ®

Mix all ingredients together to make a spicy dressing.

Blanch the squid in boiling water until done.

Mix the seafood with spicy dressing, toss gently.

Add onion and celery, and toss again.

ground roasted rice	spring onion	mint leaf
shallot	lime	coriander

Lap Kai
(Savory Chopped Chicken Salad)

Chopped chicken mixed with shallots, spring onions, lime juice, chilies, fish sauce and ground roasted rice, served with fresh vegetables. Originally from the Northeastern region of Thailand.

Preparation

Ingredients

(for 2 persons)

1½	cups	chicken, finely diced
2	tbsp	chopped spring onion
1	tbsp	chopped coriander
2	tbsp	mint leaves
2	tbsp	sliced shallot
1/2	tsp	dried chili flakes
1	tbsp	ground roasted rice
1/2	tsp	salt
2	tbsp	fish sauce (see p. 11)
2	tbsp	lime juice

Fresh vegetables: long beans, spring onion and Chinese cabbage

Garnish: mint sprig, dried chilies, spring onion, Chinese cabbage and sliced shallot

- Dry-fry the chicken in a pan using no oil and adding only a pinch of salt.
- When done, transfer chicken to a mixing bowl, season with chili flakes, fish sauce and lime juice, mix well, add ground rice and stir.
- Add spring onions, shallots, mint leaves and coriander and toss well.
- Spoon onto a serving dish, garnish with mint sprig, dried chilies, spring onion, Chinese cabbage and shallots. Serve with long beans, spring onions and cabbage.

JASMINE RICE

ASIAN BEST ® BRAND

Sprinkle the chopped chicken with salt and mix well.

Dry-fry the chicken until cooked through.

Mix the fried chicken with other ingredients, stir well.

Add spring onions, shallots, mint leaves and coriander leaves, stir.

green papaya   dried shrimp   Thai chili

garlic   long bean   roasted peanut

Som Tum
(Spicy Papaya Salad)

Papaya salad, a traditional Thai dish from the Northeastern region. A favorite served with sticky rice, grilled chicken and spicy grilled beef.

Ingredients   (for 2 persons)

2 ½	cups	shredded green papaya or carrot
1-3		Thai chilies
1	tbsp	garlic
1/4	cup	ground dried shrimp
1 ½		limes
1	tbsp	ground roasted peanuts
1	tbsp	palm sugar (see p. 11)
1	tbsp	tamarind juice (see p. 10)
1 ½	tbsp	fish sauce (see p. 11)
Fresh vegetables:		Chinese watercress, cabbage and long beans
Garnish:		cabbage and lime zest

Preparation

- Wash and peel the lime. Finely scrape the rind to obtain about 1 tablespoon of zest. Squeeze the lime to obtain 2 tablespoons of juice.
- Pound garlic and chili together.
- Add papaya and mix with the chili mixture from step 2. Season with palm sugar, fish sauce, tamarind juice and lime juice. Add 2 tablespoons of dried shrimp and combine well. Serve on a dish, sprinkle with lime zest, the remaining dried shrimp and ground roasted peanuts. Delicious with Chinese watercress, cabbage and long bean.

Blend chili and garlic together.

Mix the shredded papaya with the mixture until well mixed.

Add dried shrimp, stir well.

Sprinkle with ground roasted peanuts.

JASMINE RICE

ASIAN BEST BRAND

●●)))) EASTLAND
Serving the Best

spring roll sheet   plum sauce   bean thread

cabbage   carrot   crabmeat

Porpia Tod
(Thai Spring Rolls)

A roll stuffed with bean thread, minced pork or chicken and vegetables. A popular appetizer or snack in homes and restaurants. Serve with plum sauce.

Ingredients

		(for 4 persons)
1	cup	bean thread (see p. 11)
1	lb	spring roll sheets
7	oz	minced pork or chicken
3	oz	crabmeat
1		egg
1/2	cup	shredded cabbage
1/2	cup	shredded carrot
1/3	cup	shredded soaked
		ear mushrooms
1	tbsp	chopped garlic
1/2	tbsp	black pepper
1	tbsp	thin soy sauce (see p. 11)
4	cups	cooking oil, for deep-frying
3	tbsp	cooking oil, for stir-frying
Garnish:		spring onion tips 3"-4" long,
		sprig of sweet basil

Sauce

1/2	cup	plum sauce

JASMINE RICE

ASIAN BEST ® BRAND

Preparation

- Soak bean thread until soft, drain and cut into short lengths. Mix the pork (or chicken), crabmeat, egg, cabbage, carrot, mushrooms, pepper and soy sauce together. Add bean thread and mix well.
- In a pan sauté the garlic with 3 tbsp of oil until fragrant, add the mixture in step 1 and stir-fry until done. Set aside to cool.
- Spread a spring roll sheet on a flat surface, place 2 tbsp of the filling from step 2 on the sheet, fold the sheet to cover the filling tightly, seal the edge with the batter. Heat the oil over medium-low. Deep-fry *Porpia* until crispy and golden, remove from oil using slotted spoon and leave to cool on paper towels.
- Arrange on a serving dish, garnish with spring onion tips and sweet basil. Serve hot with plum sauce.

Tip: *The batter is made from 2 tbsp of wheat flour and 1/4 cup of water. Stir over low heat until the batter is done and clear, remove from the heat.*

Mix the minced pork, crabmeat, cabbage, carrot, mushrooms, pepper, salt and soy sauce together. Add bean thread and toss well.

Sauté the mixture with fried garlic over medium heat until done and let it cool for filling.

Fold both sides of the spring roll sheet, tightly and seal with the thick batter.

Deep-fry the Porpia in hot oil over medium-low heat until golden, remove and drain.

 EastLand
Serving the Best

48

egg

kaffir lime leaf

salt

long bean

red curry paste

sugar

Tod Mun Pla
(Fried Fish Cake)

Deep-fried ground fish with chili paste served with a cucumber relish. A delicious appetizer from the central region of Thailand.

Ingredients

Preparation

* Put all ingredients in a bowl and mix well. Knead and toss the mixture until it becomes stiff.
* Shape the mixture into small patties about 2" in diameter using 2 tbsp of mixture per patty. Deep-fry in hot oil over medium heat until golden brown. Remove from the oil and place on paper towels.
* Arrange on a serving dish, garnish with sliced pineapple. Serve with cucumber relish.

Cucumber Relish

* Clean cucumbers and cut into thin slices.
* Mix vinegar, sugar and salt together, simmer over medium heat until the sugar and salt has dissolved and the sauce has thickened slightly. Remove from the heat and allow to cool. Before serving, pour the sauce over the cucumbers and sprinkle chopped corianders, sliced red chili and sliced shallots on top.

Ingredients (for 2 persons)

1	lb	Spanish mackerel, minced
1	tbsp	canned red curry paste (see p. 10)
1		egg
1/2	cup	finely sliced long beans
3	tbsp	finely shredded kaffir lime leaves
1	tsp	salt
1	tsp	sugar
3	cups	cooking oil, for deep-frying
Garnish:		slices of pineapple

Cucumber Relish

1		finely sliced red spur chili
4		cucumbers
2		finely sliced shallots
1	tbsp	chopped coriander
1/4	tsp	salt
2	tsp	sugar
1 1/3	cups	vinegar

JASMINE RICE

ASIAN BEST BRAND

Mix all the ingredients together by hand, knead and toss against the bowl until stiff.

Make small patties about 2" in diameter.

Deep-fry in hot oil over medium heat until golden and done.

Remove from the oil and serve with cucumber relish.

garlic

Thai chili

tamarind juice

coriander root

shallot

palm sugar

Ingredients (for 3 persons)

1		whole sea bass (17 oz)
4	cups	vegetable oil
Garnish:		coriander sprigs and red spur chilies

Sauce

5		Thai chilies
1	tbsp	sliced garlic
1	tsp	chopped coriander roots
1	tbsp	palm sugar (see p. 11)
2	tbsp	fish sauce (see p. 11)
3	tbsp	tamarind juice (see p. 10)
2	tbsp	vegetable oil

JASMINE RICE

ASIAN BEST BRAND ®

Pla Rad Phrik
(Fried Sea Bass with Sweet Chili Sauce)

Crisp-fried sea bass topped with a spicy, sour and sweet sauce blending of garlic, chili, tamarind juice and sugar. One of the most popular dishes in Thailand.

Preparation

- Remove the scales from the fish and discard the insides; wash thoroughly.
- Heat the oil in a pan over medium heat. Fry fish until golden. Remove from the pan and drain off the excess oil.
- To make the sauce, mix chilies, garlic and coriander roots together. Fry in hot oil over medium heat until fragrant. Season with tamarind juice, fish sauce and sugar. Pour over the fish, garnish with coriander sprigs and chilies.

Fry the fish until golden.

Chop Thai chilies, garlic, and coriander roots together.

Fry the chopped mixture until fragrant.

Season with tamarind juice and sugar.

 EastLand
Serving the Best

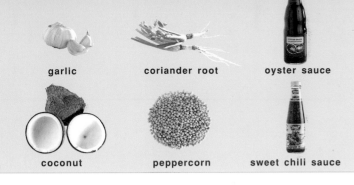

garlic   coriander root   oyster sauce

coconut   peppercorn   sweet chili sauce

Kai Yang
(Thai-Style Grilled Chicken)

Broiled chicken marinated with coriander roots, garlic, salt, pepper and coconut milk. Originally from the northeastern region of Thailand. Usually served with sticky rice, spicy papaya salad and savory chopped chicken salad.

Preparation

- To make the dipping sauce: Combine the dried chili flakes, palm sugar, fish sauce, lime juice and ground roasted rice and mix well. Sprinkle with chopped coriander, spring onion and mint leaves.
- Wash the chicken, split, open and remove the insides. Wash again.
- Blend coriander roots, garlic, salt and peppercorns in a blender. Rub the paste on both sides of the chicken.
- Mix coconut milk, soy sauce and oyster sauce together to get a marinade.
- Marinate the chicken for 2 hours.
- Grill chicken over low heat until golden and cooked through. Chop grilled chicken and arrange on a serving dish. Garnish with red and green chilies. Serve with the dipping sauce and cooked jasmine or sticky rice.

Ingredients
(for 4 persons)

1		whole chicken (2 1/4 lb)
1	cup	coconut milk
10		peppercorns
3	tbsp	minced garlic
1	tbsp	minced coriander roots
2	tbsp	oyster sauce (see p. 11)
3	tbsp	thin soy sauce (see p. 11)
1/2	tsp	salt
Garnish:		red and green spur chilies

Sauce

2	tsp	roasted dried chili flakes
1	tbsp	spring onion and coriander, finely chopped
2	tbsp	mint leaves
1	tbsp	ground roasted rice
1	tsp	palm sugar (see p. 11)
1/4	cup	lime juice
1/4	cup	fish sauce (see p. 11)

JASMINE RICE

ASIAN BEST BRAND ®

Clean the chicken, discard the insides.

Combine coriander roots, garlic, salt and pepper in the blender.

Add coconut milk into the mixture.

Grill chicken over low heat until golden.

● ●)))) EASTLAND
Serving the Best

cumin | galangal | turmeric powder
lemon grass | coriander seed | peanut sauce

Ingredients

(for 2 persons)

1	lb	pork loin, cut thinly into 1"x2" strips
1/4	tsp	roasted coriander seed powder
1/4	tsp	roasted cumin seed powder
2	tbsp	minced garlic
1/4	tsp	pepper
1/4	tsp	turmeric powder
3		sliced galangal
1	tsp	chopped lemon grass
1	tsp	salt
2	tsp	sugar
1/2	cup	coconut milk
1	cup	peanut sauce (see p. 10)
		wooden skewer

Cucumber Relish

(see p. 50)

JASMINE RICE

ASIAN BEST BRAND ®

Moo Satay
(Thai-Style Pork BBQ)

Grilled pork marinated with Thai seasoning served with spicy peanut sauce. A delightful appetizer.

Preparation

- Blend the coriander seed powder, cumin seed powder, pepper and tumeric powder with galangal, lemon grass, garlic and salt using a blender.
- Combine pork, sugar and the mixture from step 1 with the coconut milk and marinate for 1 hour.
- Thread the pork slices onto the skewers.
- Boil the marinade sauce in a pot until slightly thickened.
- Grill pork on medium heat and brush the marinade sauce onto the pork.
- Serve with peanut sauce and cucumber relish.

Cucumber Relish

- Wash and slice cucumbers.
- Mix vinegar, sugar and salt together, simmer over medium heat until the sugar and salt has dissolved and the sauce has thickened slightly. Remove from the heat and allow to cool. Before serving, pour the sauce over the cucumbers and sprinkle chopped coriander, chili and shallots on top.

Blend coriander, cumin, pepper, turmeric, galangal, lemon grass, garlic and salt together.

Pour the mixture into coconut milk, add sugar and pork slices.

Thread Moo Satay slices onto the skewers.

Grill Moo Satay on medium heat and brush on the marinade sauce.

shrimp

egg

banana blossom

rice noodles

bean sprout

Chinese chives

Pad Thai Kung Sod
(Fried Noodles with Shrimps)

Everyone's favorite noodle dish. Stir-fried noodles with shrimps, egg and chili flakes garnished with ground peanuts, bean sprouts, Chinese chives and banana blossoms.

Ingredients

Preparation

- Soak rice noodles in warm water for 2-3 minutes, or until soft.
- Clean the shrimps.
- Fry shallots and garlic in 2 tbsp of oil over medium heat until fragrant. Add palm sugar, tamarind juice and fish sauce; stir together. Remove and set aside.
- Heat 2 tbsp of oil in a pan, add beaten eggs and stir until the eggs are almost set, add shrimps and sauté until done. Add rice noodles, stir for 2-3 minutes and pour the sauce over and stir again. Follow with bean sprouts and Chinese chives and continue stirring for 2 more minutes.
- Spoon onto a serving dish, sprinkle with roasted peanuts and chili flakes. Serve with banana blossom, fresh bean sprouts, Chinese chives and lime wedge.

Ingredients (for 2 persons)

3½	oz	thin dried rice noodles (see p. 11)
6		shrimps
2		eggs
2	cups	bean sprouts
1/4	cup	Chinese chives, cut lengthwise
1	tbsp	chopped garlic
1	tbsp	sliced shallot
2	tsp	chili flakes
2	tbsp	ground roasted peanuts
2	tbsp	palm sugar (see p. 11)
2	tbsp	tamarind juice (see p. 10)
2	tbsp	fish sauce (see p. 11)
4	tbsp	vegetable oil

Fresh vegetables: banana blossom, bean sprouts, Chinese chives and lime wedge

JASMINE RICE

ASIAN BEST BRAND ®

Fry shallots and garlic together, add tamarind juice.

Fry eggs with shrimps until done.

Add noodles and pour the sauce over.

Add bean sprouts and Chinese chives, continue frying for few more minutes.

 EastLand
Serving the Best

garlic | holy basil leaf | Thai chili

flat noodles | fish sauce | sweet soy sauce

Kuaytiew Pad Khi Mao Kai
(Spicy Fried Noodles with Chicken)

Pan-fried flat noodles with Thai chilies, garlic, fresh basil leaves and chicken. The real taste of a Thai lunch.

Ingredients

Preparation

10½	oz	flat noodles	
7	oz	chicken breast, cut into bite-size pieces	
1/2	cups	holy basil leaves	
1/2	tsp	chopped Thai chili	
1	tbsp	chopped garlic	
1½	tbsp	fish sauce (see p. 11)	
1	tsp	sugar	
1	tsp	sweet soy sauce	
3	tbsp	vegetable oil	
Garnish:		crisp-fried holy basil leaves and Thai chilies	

(for 2 persons)

- Toss the flat noodles with sweet soy sauce.
- Heat oil in a pan over medium heat and fry the chili and garlic together until fragrant.
- Add chicken and fry until done. Add noodles and fry for a further 2-3 minutes.
- Season with fish sauce and sugar. Add the holy basil leaves and stir well.
- Garnish with holy basil leaves and Thai chilies. Serve hot.

Thoroughly mix the noodles with sweet soy sauce.

Stir-fry garlic and chili until fragrant.

Fry the chicken with the mixture until done.

Add the noodles, stir well. Then sprinkle some holy basil leaves.

JASMINE RICE

ASIAN BEST ® BRAND

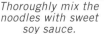 **EastLand**
Serving the Best

Asian Best Jasmine Rice

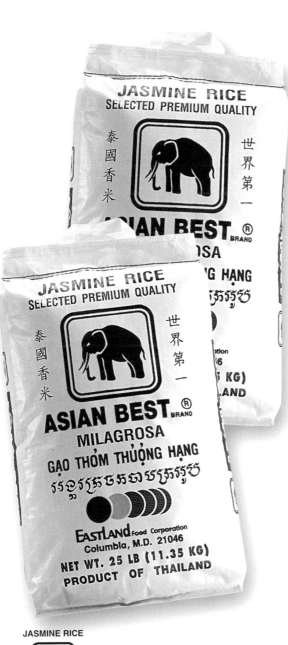

JASMINE RICE
ASIAN BEST®

Eastland Food Corporation and Chia Meng Co., Ltd.

Eastland is a fully integrated importer and distributor of consumer products, bringing the very best from the Orient to the U.S.A. The company's policy is to supply the best products available by dealing only with the best producers in Asia and maintaining the highest standards of quality. As a consequence of this policy, the company's premium quality jasmine rice, marketed under the brand name Asian Best, enjoys a major presence in the U.S. market.

Eastland in partnership with the Chia Meng Co., Ltd., a top processor of jasmine rice, supplies 100% pure jasmine rice to the U.S. market. Chia Meng, with facilities located in the heart of Thailand's jasmine rice bowl, has been in the business for over six decades and, unlike other producers, mills, polishes, refines and packages only jasmine and no other white rice. With emphasis on quality, from selection to packaging, Chia Meng consistently delivers the highest quality jasmine rice and has, over the years, gained a well earned reputation as Thailand's leading producer of the world's finest jasmine rice.

Chia Meng produces over 700 tons of rice per day using state of the art equipment including a climate controlled silo and an ultra modern, fully automated and environmentally friendly mill. The company is an ISO 9002 and 14000 accredited company and produces to HACCP, WTO CODEX and SQF quality standards. The company has been granted many other awards including Thai Hom Mali Rice certification from the Thai Department of Foreign Trade, the International Asia Award and the Thai Prime Minister's awards for Export and Industry Environmental Management Systems.

Products Recommended by Eastland

Asian Best Canned
Products

Maesri Chili Paste
Products

Golden Mountain
Seasoning Sauce Products

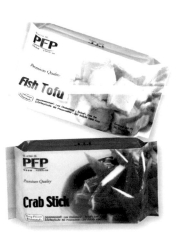

Coco King Coconut
Products

PFP Seafood
Products

Oyster Brand
Fish Sauce

BDMP Dehydrated
Seafood Products

Healty Boy Soy Sauce
Products

Hand Brand No. 1
Spice and Herb Products

S&P Frozen Dishes
and Pastry Products

RED CURRY PASTE
(Nam Phrik Kaeng Daeng)

5		dried red spur chilies, seeded and soaked
5		shallots, sliced
10	cloves	garlic
1	tsp	galangal, finely sliced
1	tbsp	lemon grass, sliced
1	tsp	kaffir lime rind, finely sliced
2	tsp	chopped coriander root
5		peppercorns
1	tbsp	ground roasted coriander seed
1	tsp	roasted cumin
1	tsp	salt
1	tsp	shrimp paste

- Pound together coriander seeds, cumin and peppercorns to obtain a fine paste. Spoon into a bowl and put aside.
- Pound dried chilies and salt thoroughly, add galangal, lemon grass, kaffir lime rind, coriander roots, garlic, shallots and pound well.
- Add the cumin mixture, follow with shrimp paste. pound until everything is well-combined.

KHAO MOK KAI SAUCE
(Nam Jim Khao Mok Kai)

1	tbsp	red and green Thai chilies, diced
1/4	cup	mint leaves, chopped
2	tbsp	spring onion, chopped
2	tbsp	coriander leaves, chopped
1	tsp	salt
1/2	cup	sugar
1/2	cup	vinegar

- Finely chop the mint leaves, spring onion, coriander leaves and chilies.
- Mix the vinegar, sugar and salt together, stir over medium heat until lightly thickened.
- Remove from heat, add chopped vegetables and mix thoroughly.

SOUR CURRY PASTE
(Nam Phrik Kaeng Som)

3		dried red spur chilies, seeded and soaked
5	bulbs	shallots, sliced
3	cloves	garlic
1/2	tbsp	shrimp paste
1/2	tsp	salt
1/2	cup	cooked fish meat
1	tbsp	wild ginger

- Pound or blend in a blender until a fine paste is formed.
- Add cooked fish meat and pound well.

GREEN CURRY PASTE
(Nam Phrik Kaeng Khiew Wan)

10		large green hot chilies
3		shallots, sliced
9	cloves	garlic
1	tsp	finely sliced galangal
1	tbsp	sliced lemon grass
1/2	tsp	finely sliced kaffir lime rind
1	tsp	chopped coriander root
5		peppercorns
1	tbsp	roasted coriander seeds
1	tsp	roasted cumin
1	tsp	salt
1	tsp	shrimp paste

- Combine coriander seeds, cumin and peppercorns in a mortar, pound well. Transfer to a bowl and set aside.
- Pound hot chilies and salt together. Add the remaining ingredients except shrimp paste. Pound until mixed well.
- Add the cumin mixture and shrimp paste and continue pounding until smooth and fine.

JASMINE RICE

ASIAN BEST